DIMENSIONS

SHAHIDAH JANJUA

SHAHIDAH JANJUA

Published by Geepy Publishing 2014

Copyright © 2014 Shahidah Janjua

The moral rights of the author has been asserted

All rights reserved.

No part of this publication may be reproduced, stored in a retrieval system, or transmitted in any form by any means, without the prior permission in writing of the publisher, nor be otherwise circulated in any form of binding or cover other than that in which it is published and without a similar condition including this condition being imposed on the subsequent purchaser

Geepy Publishing
Ireland
www.geepypublishing.com

ISBN-13: 978-0-9927564-3-7

SHAHIDAH JANJUA

CONTENTS

Dedication

Family	3
Belonging	6
Wall	8
Trace of Silver	10
Grief	12
The Adam Diaries	14
Seismic Shifts	17
Atoms	18
Playful Panthers are Perfect	20
Wild	21
Echo	24
A Promise	28

DIMENSIONS

Listen up you Feckers	30
Carolina	32
Bedlam	34
Freedom	36
Language	39
Not Tangible Enough	42
Dust to Dust	44
Daring to Cross the Ages	47
Romeo	49
A History	52
Thoughts for the Day	54
The Hurricane	57
The Lost City	60

SHAHIDAH JANJUA

DEDICATION

For all the brave women past and present who have given me the words to speak my truths. A special dedication to Andrea Dworkin for her wisdom and vision. She taught me plain speaking and truth telling. A special thank you to my partner, my mate, for an enduring belief in me and respect for my creative work.

SHAHIDAH JANJUA

Family

I was birthed into an intimate space
Shared by two other women.
In the long view
Telescoping back through the years
Of many severed moments,
Dislocations of time and meaning
Displacement of bodies from here to there
From there to here.
I see our intimacy
Was only a matter of geography.
Tropics and contours fixing us on a line
Bordered by nation, clan and family.

From large peasant beginnings
In sprawling fields, chasing clouds
Through the broad village maze,
To the dung laced alleyways,
The origins of pebble dash
In downtown ghetto quarters Lahore.

We were moulded in the same
Rich warm odour of cowpat mixture
Straw-manure - for nourishment and fire.
Each body and soul intact
Welded together for breath
And sweat and labour.

Falling loose from the nipple too soon
I did not know
The meaning of my hunger
'Til there was too much loneliness
In the world
Sitting outside the fraternities
Of feasting, drinking revelling
We were never meant to gel
Only in the sisterhood of servitude.
Our time together mediated
By the fathers wants, the brothers needs
The husbands will, the suitors gaze.

I came this far with sisters who
Were not the gene connection.

Sometimes without a word link
Women small and tall,
Broad and slender, masked unmasked.
I chose from amongst them
Companions for the journeying way
But I carry them all with me.
The razored leg, the high heeled foot
The stubbled chin,
Choosing my family
Keeping the rest of womankind in view.

Belonging

The bread maker squats beside her earth oven. Grandmother has asked me to take our dough balls to her, so that she can cook them in time for our dinner. I have no idea of the time. I only know it is late in the day, and the others will be arriving soon from their work in the fields. We will all sit around the fire in the courtyard, and eat together.

Earlier in the day I had carried the pitcher down to the stream, to fill it with water for grandmother. While I was at the stream I met Zohra and Aisha, who were washing their clothes. They were banging them; bashing them on the rocks, to get the dirt out. Their actions had a rhythm. Swing the clothes up in the air, high above the head, then bring them crashing down onto the rocks. Down, up, crash. Down, up, crash. Clothes and bodies swaying, as they sang to the rhythm of the latest hits of Lata Mangeshkar. Their voices like mountain flutes.

I watched and listened, for I don't know how long. Lost in those moments. Lost in that rhythm; in the sound of the voices; in the flow of the water. Humming the tunes; making my own refrains.

The bread maker is deeper voiced, from years

of smoking her hookah. She is singing the old songs, lilting, haunting, so sad. Her rhythm is slower. She peels off a slice of the uncooked dough from the top of the pile. Swings it gently towards the oven, down into it, and slaps the dough on to the side, then she peels off the cooked bread. She throws it in the air, and it lands with a slap on a pile of cooked unleavened bread. She gently covers them with her brilliant white cloth. Up, forward, down, slap, up, down, rest. Up, forward, down, slap, up, down, rest. The bread maker is Zubeida with the grey eyes. She has a few yellow teeth. Her skin is like the earth before the monsoon comes. Her smile is the red ribbon around my heart. She is beautiful. This is my home.

Wall

The wall marked the beginning of the playground, which was anywhere and everywhere beyond our courtyard through which the clouds would drift, my grandmother making a show of shooing them away to entertain me. She was awesome with her toothless smile and craggy face, its crevices dark with memories. I'd trace them with small fingers and get lost in that maze.

I strolled along the top of the wall with the skill of a tightrope walker, my cousin's eyes agog at my daring. I'd named him aloo, potato, for his shiny hairless head. He wore a bright red coat, which had arrived in some Oxfam consignment, from a far off land where people had clothes to give away. From the top of the wall he looked like a butterfly fluttering along the ground.

My mother told me there was a horizon beyond that wall. I remember it as the trees casting shadows on the sun as it sought to rise above the ground. My sun came suddenly at midday – sometimes. Within the walls of the courtyard there were, at times, impenetrable walls, walls of silence where there was nothing visible to climb. There could be erected at a whim. You could be skipping along coming in from having fetched water from the mountain stream, or taking dough to the woman with the oven in the ground who would magic it into bread. You could be coming back from morning class which happened under the tree at edge of the village, bringing your slate and chalk home to show off your mastery of the Urdu alphabet, or returning from the fields where you had helped to harvest the wheat, and bang you'd hit this invisible wall just inside the front door and a dread would grip your heart, wondering if you had helped to erect it but couldn't remember the how or the why or the what of it. And you'd learn to think what of it, and go skipping out again in the hope that it would be gone by the time you came back.

My father lived behind a very tall wall which had one huge door with a small window in the middle of it. If you spoke nicely to the man with the big bunch of keys and showed him some papers he would unlock the huge door and let you in. My father had one room and there were bars on his windows. When I saw him he could come out in his courtyard and play games with me. Our favourite was blind man's bluff.

Trace of Silver

She was a homeopath.
There is no lasting herstory
Of her powers of healing.
She saved my arm
From a life of limp uselessness,
When the experts had long given up.

How could she have borne,
Bearing eleven children.
His abandonment, her incestuous sons.
A daughter of fourteen married
Into sexual slavery to the raja
With stuck together eyes,
From too much drinking

Six daughters, three homes,
She moves between them,
Leaving a trace of silver in each.
Leaving the scent of lavender,

Leaving hearts and bodies

Made whole again.

By the touches beyond tenderness.

By the voice like bird song.

She comforts me, still

Grief
For Adam

Grief is a note here and there
At a pitch that tears the heart
Grief is in a sonata or a song
'Heart on my sleeve' he sings tunefully
But I know mine lies in tatters – my sleeve, my heart
Hanging by a thread from my breastbone.

Grief is on the beach where we left our footprints
in the sand, made up of a million crushed particles -
the sand, my heart -
For the duration of the changing tides
When all trace of us was washed away

Grief is in the photographs you took
of the rocks resembling dinosaur bones
Relics of many eons past
Now rooted through the shingle to the clay

below
Where I search you out, whilst you keep company with strangers

Grief spills into the cracks in the earth
More viscous than blood, more precious than water,
It frames the rainbow in a luminescent sky
My spirit lays down, its cheek pressed to the velvet grass
While my body goes about its daily business

The Adam Diaries

March 6th 2013

It is 2 years and six months since you died. The word 'dead' still does not sit comfortably with me. You and I never believed in 'death'. Just days before you left, we had spoken about how the world is a closed system that nothing comes into or leaves. I think in retrospect we meant the universe. When the remains of comets land here, or pieces of asteroids, I think of you as the atoms and molecules you are now and your travels across the universe and indeed to all the places on this planet, that you had hoped to see but had not, while your heart was still beating. It required a stillness that you had not yet achieved. And although your atoms speed from place to place it is with an inner calm that this planet would never allow you.

I hope this sometimes sense of anguish I have about not having been a good enough friend as a mother, dissipates over time. It does get in the way of having a conversation with you of the type we liked best; our favoured latest reads, a worthwhile film, scientific theories, motivational people. We might phone to simply hear each other's voices; make the cursory enquiry about health, peace of mind, work, relationships and we'd quickly move from these to all the larger than life ideas that usually occupied us.

Hugo Chavez died yesterday and I am saddened by humanity's loss of him. Perhaps you have already joined each other in that way that kind souls do, to undertake a different journey, one that I have not yet imagined, or am unable to while bound by the weight of flesh and blood and rooted by the force of gravity. I remember that Einstein could be wrong, specifically about the latter, as he was about so much else. I do imagine that the sum of all we know is but a dew drop in this morning of your new found existence.

March 7th 2013

Now that I have found a way of talking with you my mind dwells on the possibility of an ongoing conversation. Last night my dreams were suffused with what words we would say next, and next, and thereafter. It was an endless stream until I awoke in the early hours. What I am really grateful for is that you have left all the disturbances behind; the thoughts with jagged edges, the ones you tried to drown in the alcohol you hated, which was the means to that end and no pleasure in itself. I believe you tried to create communities of belonging based on your very varied interests and talents. And it all seemed to come together when we talked, your words 'It was lovely talking with you', were your gift to me, now more than ever.

March 8th 2013

It is International Women's Day my son. Not a day we would ordinarily have shared with each other, but one which I know you tried to honour in your living. It is only when the drink took hold and ran you ragged, that the lines between your best thoughts and your worst nightmares became blurred. It was so tragic and heart-breaking to watch you, the gentlest of human beings, brought so low that you could not, for one moment, consider forgiving yourself. There was no coming back, you said, from buying a woman, who you wanted to find again in order to make an abject apology. Instead you lay on the tiled floor of my kitchen trying to pull your hair out with the pain and grief of it all, knowing there was no excuse, that it was a choice you had made at one fateful moment.

Seismic Shifts

Slow grind of tectonic plates

Sleeping dinosaurs shifting

The flutter of a heart

A missed beat

Cold fissures in the earth

Swallow birdsong

Silence erupts

The surface splits

And at the core

Heartbreak

Atoms

Three years now since we laid you there
Amongst the many others who left too soon
Across the path in the space bordered by trees
Lay the children
I wanted you to be with them, my child

Some mornings I awake and know
You touched me in the night
Your atoms danced around my heart

Some days I see you on a rainbow
On a seagulls' wing
With the heron as it ascends
The finches at the feeder

You saw the beauty in everything
Even Geiger's drawings of the Alien
The world was a wondrous place

DIMENSIONS

Three years now since we laid you there

And you have risen to travel the universe

Sitting on the edge of black holes

Making friends with quarks

Hurtling through the hadron collider

You are out there

You are in there

And in here

Your atoms dancing around my heart

Playful Panthers are Perfect

If panthers can be perceptive, poor
Pakistani, and positively potty.
Then I could be one.
If panthers can be confident, colourful
Considerate and confused.
Then maybe I am one.
If panthers can be artistic, analytical
Active and angry.
I quite possibly am one.
If panthers are brave and black,
Then, all modesty aside,
We're a perfect match.

Wild

Wild were the blackberries I picked. Their juices bleeding purple through my fingers turning them into baby egg plants. This wildness feeds my body and fills my soul.

I was always the wild child, defying conventions, disobeying every rule "Put in place for my safety", so they said. The wild white horse agreed with me. She told me so when she galloped through the market while I clung to her naked back, stitched there like a small brown parcel, while she hoofed the oranges out of the way, made mush of the mangoes, and snorted over the spice stall covering us both in a multi-coloured dust.

"That was wild altogether, sir", said my good friend in his gruff County Derry accent, when I told him the story. I told my friend a story I had read in The Book of Quantum Mythology in which the most eminent scientists had been driven to a wild despair when faced with overwhelming evidence that Einstein was plain wrong. Oh, he had been grand at knowing what he saw – the amazing order of things, tiny seedlings growing into giant sequoias, the house that Jack built out of their wood, the pears falling off the trees in autumn, and William's arrow travelling in a straight line every time he split the apple which sat wobbling on his own son's head.

With that same confidence did Einstein create his rules for life the universe and everything, because he couldn't conceive of what he could not see. Below the surface there is a wild dance of atoms, neutrons and quarks, which inhabit every seemingly vacant space. They are the life-blood of dark matter and cannot be captured in a mathematical formula, or become the rote for the daily 9 to 5 grind of city life. Any wild child could have told him how wrong he was to impose an order on things beyond his meagre human imagination, but no one was listening.

So the wild solar storms go on, up there in the unseen realms of our very small solar system, pushing and pulling at the ionosphere. When the storms stop raging the heat settles over the polar ice caps and they melt into its warm embrace.

And if bombing the moon, as they did last week, proves or disproves the existence of water on her already pock marked skin, so what. The waters here are rising, and people are fleeing the flooded plains around the rivers of Bangladesh. Part of the beach at Rossbeigh has been swallowed by the sea and broken the circular track around that hallowed coastline, which had harboured the souls of its fishermen.

Wild became feral when big people who had forgotten who they once were broke the hearts of their sons with the indignity of this naming, and with false promises of health, wealth and happiness to be attained without the grace of labour. It is with wild abandon that feral children had skipped into the world eager to learn and love and trust.

Echo

My playful side ever present, pops out like the naughty pixie that it is, around the jagged edges of any issue, any conflict or conundrum. The pixie embodies my optimism. There is an echo of someone saying that I would be optimistic even while I stood at the gates of hell. It was not a compliment. Thankfully pixies are not deterred by real world referents. So do I even need to say that in that playful realm echo became Decco, one of the formidable players in my favoured football team.

When everyone sits down to watch the match, the sport, ganged up in sometimes not so friendly rivalry, I sit down to watch a classical ballet of pirouettes and pas de deux's, of spins and flicks and slight of foot and hand of course – very topical since Henri's touch. I watch the dance, which reaches a crescendo in every goal scored, the ball aimed and struck with exquisite finesse and an almighty power that could leave a hole where the goalkeeper's guts had been. The chants and taunts are echoes of ancient rivalries and tribal warfare.

No one said that ballet wasn't violent. It crucifies the toes and arches of once delicately moulded feet, their metatarsals forged together to an impossible purpose. The tortured feet are echoes of those bound into lotus shapes then drenched in rose water to disguise the stink of rotting flesh. Well-to-do Chinese women hobbled on them inelegantly through all the years of their dutiful lives.

At the behest of Uncle Mao as he was known in our village, and his fellow long marchers, men and women, friends of peasants, righters of wrongs, the bandages were unfurled from a million feet. There was enough stinking cloth to wrap around the belly of the earth over and over again.

Cloth bears echoes of the drapery that makes shapeless forms of otherwise curvaceous women in Afghanistan, the dutiful daughters of some other fathers in tribal settings, where football stadiums are scenes of a carelessly choreographed dance of death; stonings and beheadings, in which, in true Brechtian style, the audience is invited to participate. Would that we watchers had all just lost our heads to that miserable plot.

Here are echoes of theatre and the awful irony of Theatres of War, highly technologised affairs, but only road shows, where locality dictates the props and settings and these are secondary to the action, always far from here. Here is where the audience watches with breathless anticipation and anxiety, some fearful for their loved ones, whoever's side they're on, some oblivious to the secondary plot contrived by the dieux et machina who rewrote the lexicon we thought we had all understood, until now. My pixie tells me writers are warriors of a kind, going back to the words, studying and honing the craft, preserving the lexicon and guarding its meaning. I am truly blessed by her presence.

DIMENSIONS

A Promise

The finest and most cherished love
from the will to freedom
yours and mine.
To honour beyond words
And into languages each other's souls –
Shukriya

You bring wisdom
and the ancient ways
in your sturdy bones,
the pride and stealth
Of Amazons - stalking jaguar
to share our wildness with
in a jungle frolic.

We will move from
continent to continent
with agile grace and ease.
Will cut through flesh

to the heart
with a single gaze
In search of truth.
And then to speak it.

Seekers in the sub-terrain.
Digging deep near magma – unafraid.
Finding the cords that bind us
to her navel earth – mother.
Where all the evidence lies
That we are She,
too wise too present and too urgent
to be vanquished - ever.

Drawing the circle to a close
Bare breasted and large hipped
we will arrive in the near future.
Never to submerge again.

Listen up you Feckers

My daughter Bridget
Went missing last night.
Out in 10 inch heels
And a boob tube around her arse.
I didn't know she was gone
Until I looked in her bedroom.
You'd think it was the local landfill site
But there were no signs of life
Not human ones anyway.

"Oh my God", I was in a state
Of sheer panic, my heart shredded.
"She's been kidnapped, sold off
On the white slave market.
Trafficked for prostitution.
She could be anywhere – Thailand
Colombia, Brazil, Amsterdam
Phone the Gardaí NOW." I tell myself
Hands shaking, and I've nearly wet me

knickers.

The mobile rings before I can
It's Bridget –
"So sorry mam, I had to stay over at Cathy's.
Couldn't get a taxi.
I'll be home soon, so sorry.
Mam, mam, are you there?
Me tongue is glued to the
Roof of me mouth.
I prise it down and whisper
"Yes love, fine love, just get back"
So listen up you feckers
I'm chucking that telly out and
All the bad news, newspapers
To keep meself sane.
Well, I'll do it after EastEnders.

Carolina

Carolina Maria de Jesus you were with me
Though I didn't know your name
In my flat beneath the laundry
With its one eyed window
Looking out onto stairs descending
Into that airless hell.

It held the cries of my two babies
From hunger and fever and a sorrow
Too big for so small a dwelling.
We rattled around
In bone clad spirits
Bumping into concrete walls
And cardboard boxes
Diarrhoea draining our lives.

My mother lived two miles up the road
A slave to two tyrants
Not oblivious to our lives

But chained by hers.
Where were the women when we needed them
But in a colonial wasteland
Which had sucked them dry of self.
If the mirror holds no reflection
Of her own face
How will she find me
Who am made in her image
My lotus feet the only mark
Of recognition.

NB: Carolina Maria de Jesus lives in a favela on the outskirts of Rio de Janiero. Her book Beyond Pity *contains extracts from her diary.*

Bedlam

Standing beside the walls of Bedlam.
I know the world is too cruel a place
for any of us to be whole.
It is said we have moved on
Spreading evenly into equality.
Our colours and our genders blurred
Into the sameness of assimilation.

I've seen the quilted arms of women.
The criss cross patterns on my own
From acts and signs of self-disgust
and a fire so raging through our veins
that only letting blood could quell it.
I am living with cold and hunger and thirst
That gnaw me in and out
While I walk abreast of the times
On my new green carpet - courtesy of the
State.
It is said I chose it.

DIMENSIONS

Like I chose to live on the outer edge,
taking with me my language and my songs.
Balancing carefully on the precipice of Being or not.
Before this I chose male lovers
in wide eyed knowledge of my stifled No's
re-enactments of rapes and pornographic poses.
I chose my children from my childhood
A catalogue of do's and don'ts
And family albums of how it ought to be.

Choosing over and over again
I chose the uncle who raped me
for his gift of literacy and history
for the chance of Nation and identity.
I have been overwhelmed by choices
In an underwhelming context.
Do I forgive myself consent
Or applaud its opportunities?

Freedom

Freedom is everywhere
And we're living happily ever after
This is not science fiction – it is now.
The Russians got into the Free Market
And Gregori's labour is worth 50 times less
Than under that nasty communism
He's a dead red
Just give him another 5 years
and his body will have freed his soul.

10 and 13 year old girls
Are skipping along the streets of Kings Cross
Not free exactly but inexpensive
£20 a fuck in a back seat or side street
Not a bad deal - riding on the backs of
6 year old girls in Thailand
Free from HIV - that is what
Civilised white western gentlemen say
Who practice safe sex with children.

DIMENSIONS

When you live up in the sky
On the enth floor of a concrete block
You should think you own the world
Instead of being the ungrateful bitch
Who cries in the park
When she feels the grass under her feet
Hears bird song and whispering trees
Since she became a freebird, skylark.

Nobody marches for freedom now
They walk to celebrate
Performing non-traditional tricks
Like being transgendered
Fancy names for men pretending - they're not
And body sculpting women who used to
Slash - but they're body beautiful now
Freed of the pain of memory.

Before freedom you made a decision
Now you take it
Pluck it out of the air

And pretend it doesn't belong to you
You freewheel across the internet
Being Al Capone or Molly Malone
Advertising your children to the paedophile
brotherhood
No one knows the real you
That's assuming you do.

Communications technology puts you in touch
With Everyone - 30, white and male
Given a few exceptions
Notably not the women of the Mekong delta
The Indus valley or the Zambezi River
Or Phillipina maids in Saudi
Who've got freed into new age slavery.

While Chipka women hug their trees
You happily eat BSE as a
Statement against bygone Nazi's
Because you're free
Because you're free
Because you're free, because you're free.

Language

Take this language and make of it
What you will
It is losing its meanings daily
Reducing to sounds across cultures
Hollow echoes in head bones
No more depths for diving
Only shallow and vague
Which cannot bathe or cleanse me
Dirt clings to rough tongues

Each word I've found to
Raise my phoenix spirit
Returns to ashes
When I have no power to hold it
I need more believing hands
To lift it into view
To keep it there a beacon
For a larger purpose.

Purpose is as purpose does
'Oppression' is old hat
Victims are unfashionable
Rights are for Rapists
Freedom is for fuckers
Justice is for Judge Clarence
Punishment is for the poor
Batterings and bombs bring us
Back to basics
Nobility is servitude
Integrity is mathematics
When will we need to weep no more.

I am choking on your strapped on dildo
Because it makes your Pride march
And makes me Linda Marciano
Terrorised into swallowing your lies
Freedom is a spit word for the gutter.

We have loved each other
To bloody battered bits
Coupled into romantic oblivion

DIMENSIONS

Rushed into singeing sunsets like lemmings
For a fleeting fucking moment
Of bodily ecstasy
Liberated into chains
Whips, welts and studded belts
Pierced prodded poked into Somebodies.
Death lies in deception.

Hear this, feel it through your pores
Taste this, touch it with your heart
The words we use never belonged to us
But meaning always did.
Use it infuse it suffuse it
With light and strength and power
Raise reckless tidal courage
Run with the wind
Come hard and tender into vision
Crack open every construction
Create yourself anew.

Not Tangible Enough

Literacy has not enabled me to speak
In words on paper of
What it is that crushes me.
This is not a hankering after ignorance
The so called age of innocence
It is the fright of recognition
That I know so much
Have read a billion words
And am bereft of knowledge
That can serve my life.

It's not that I have not
Caught glimpses of myself
Sometimes a wholesome view
Sometimes a vista or a mere scenario
That encompassed me.
Always the possibility of me
The reality of this me
Came from other women's lives.

DIMENSIONS

Their blood sweat words and brushstrokes
Wrung out on patterns across a page.

I've read enough to fill my walls
And still, and yet
For all the versions of myself
That have floated across time
In words in pictures and in myths
I am not visible to myself.
Not heard enough
Not seen enough
To form the firmer contours
Required for my recognition.
Not tangible enough to be of substance
A real flesh and heart woman
Whose blood and tears have meaning
When they spot the sheets
And fill the rivers.

Dust to Dust

There is a hunger in my belly
A hunger for feeling
A hunger for food
The pain of wanting
Bloats me so I look sated
By the roundness of my gut
Which is the deep well of my emptiness.

For need of touch and bread
Or tears and bread
My eyes glimpse images
Of patriarchal feasts
Flashing past me on TV
I have this luxury
But not the right to life.

I am a mother
Who watches a parade of death
In every worldly city

I see it through my children's eyes
Which seek the stars
As an escape route to oblivion
When crusts of mouldy bread
Do not meet their expectations

While the shops are full
Of Christmas toys
And someone said
If we were frugal
We could buy them.

I was never allowed frugality
With my optimism
Hope was ever made the woman
In nature or in nurture
So skilful at survival
With art and guile and cunning
My wiles personified as Mother Earth

But in these moments
I am dust to dust

What of my craft

When lacking seed and soil

I plant the crust

That does not make the bread tree grow

Daring to Cross the Ages

I could simply be another centenarian who receives a birthday card from the Queen, but maybe not, given that I am an immigrant, only 'naturalised', a frightening term used then, more than 40 years ago.

I could settle gracefully for hearing the 'age old' comment of 'The changes she must have lived through!' when no one actually asks what these were, what they have meant to the fabric of my own life and the lives I have witnessed being lived, by friends and family members old and new; my great grandchild is only weeks old. I could do a number of passive and dignified things that are surely befitting an older woman who to all outward appearances has sense and sanity.

In fact I am eternally grateful to all the forces that have shaped me that I always believed I had neither, sense nor sanity, until the world became a place increasingly filled with nonsense and successfully mimicking the insane.

In this instance asking would confer a degree of integrity on the subject. Asking would infer a genuine curiosity. My question is 'Do we in the enlightened west really live in conditions that entertain either, individual integrity or genuine curiosity? I challenge you to meet me on equal terms, to be mindful of the layers of age and gender stereotyping which have been laid brick upon brick to build the walls between us, indeed to be more bold than that, to engage in an endeavour to dismantle them.

The media and its critical commentators draw attention to an increasingly youth-enised culture. I can bear testimony to it, though no one is asking. But what exactly does it have to offer!

Did you get the society that you wanted?

Romeo

Romeo got so mad with his dad, he thought nothing else and nobody else could hurt him as much as his dad had. The hurt didn't show because it was on the inside, in his heart or his liver, his lungs, somewhere soft and vital, somewhere vulnerable. The skin and bones became the armour to protect it. He walked around as if he was invincible and the gang thought he was brave and exciting. His mother called it 'raging hormones' and being 'easily led'. She didn't know he was fighting to be someone, not lonely, not an only child, not dual heritage, not a fatherless son, not disowned by half his ancestry from the North West Province, the home of supposed warriors.

The gang could not lead Romeo but it could take his rage by the nose and rag it around through the gutter where the gang could hide behind him. It could 'front him up' for the things the other boys were too scared to do. He did it all with a swagger of his skinny hips, his cap pulled down to cover the 'cut in' parting in his hair and the neat nick in his eyebrow, while the fake cubic diamond in his ear threw out sparks, when lit up by the orange light of the street lamps. Romeo's memory of the beating, the hospital, the nightmares, the bruises, the sick and the sweat was gradually fading.

His luck was wearing thin. The police were forever coming banging at the door at shocking hours to check his whereabouts or search his bedroom. This time they found a stack of credit cards, and a supposed handmade explosive device that looked like something left over from the Gun Powder plot. No one could take it seriously apart from the police who used his mother's shock to insinuate several frightening scenarios. They didn't have to where his nan was concerned, she already had images of Guantanamo firmly planted in her head, and Jean Charles DeMenezez shot in the head at point blank range on the floor of a London underground station.

Romeo wanted out of the gang, his friends, the neighbourhood and his mum's constant mobile calls asking where he was. "Just up the road", was his usual reply, never specifying which road. To her there was only one 'the road', the one on which their terraced house stood. She'd stop panicking then, stop ringing friends who could make a dark drama out of a clear spring day.

It wasn't boredom, or thrills or fear that drove him now, it was a sense of dislocation and disintegration. His brain sparked with questions and ideas, when it had the chance, but with his 'street-talk' he couldn't even find the words to say them. God, the frustration, and 'What was the bloody point'? He walked into a bank, tried to use a credit card, not his, for cash. It failed, he walked out, then walked back in to try again – a suicide mission. The police caught him running down the High Street.

He sits in his cell in Juvie going over it all. There's plenty of time on your own during 12hr lock-ups. Asian lads from neighbouring towns embrace and welcome him. Some of their families are from the North West Province, where his father, who will not see him, comes from.

A History

A history of bombs and bullets
Finds us living on the surface of our skins
With wide and frightened eyes
The only snapshots in the papers
And on the mind's eye
Were of craters in the earthscape
And craters in the flesh

We got tongue-tied into silence
Living in the gut of fear
There were no hiding places left
From enemies or friends
Our inward retreat became complete
This is the stuff that jokes are made of
Laughter in the face of someone else's death
The humiliation of our poverty
We said it was survival

The wreckage that is left

Is a rubble of lies

Where do we begin to confront them

The lies you told me

The lies I told you

In order to remain Alive

In the swirls of land beneath Cavehill

      beneath Blacks Mountain

Thoughts for the Day

Walk on a knife edge
And your feet bleed
In this morning of flashbacks
Give it a fancy name
A post traumatic thingummy
Pain is pain is pain
Medicalise it analyse it
Pathologise it and puff
The magic dragon -
Didn't make it go away!

It's Belfast he's shot there's blood
His brains - splash - you're dumb
For four days
It's a post traumatic thingummy
Give it a fancy name, then
You won't have to worry about
The bigger picture.

DIMENSIONS

Put the phone down on
The phone-in that you loathe
Small voices   huge emotions
Cut dead in their prime
Insanity looms large
On this side of the picture window
Please let me get through this day
I'll deal with tomorrow- tomorrow.

Get out   take the tram be normal
Like the man with the MANIAC t-shirt
He's a moving target or am I?
The woman with hugely protruding breasts
Makes more impact on the world
Than the events that cause
Post traumatic things
It is not her decision
She's simply carrying the weight of it.

I left my skin at home
Behind the picture window

It's hard to dress for an occasion
That happened four years ago.

The Hurricane

Unbearable the weight of hatred

Tripping light-foot across

The crushed and drowned,

Slums of New Orleans

Black home of sweet music

Ravaged they say by a woman's wrath - Katrina

Neglected levees leaked money for bombs,

To kill, other souls in other lands,

Multinational, International

The planet technologised into smallness

Satellites for easy access to murder

And turning a blind white eye

A million and a million and a million

Soundless voices, sub-human

Submerged, only audible as complaint

Telling an old righteous story

Greeted with pale pity or scorn

"Oh not that again"

Looters and bombers

Black faces etched with grief and fury,

White heroes bring food, saviours bring guns

Images courtesy of Fox and CNN

Civilisation Gandhi said

"Is a good idea" for the West.

Charitable donations are welcome

For tsunamis and genocide.

Put the Euro in the box

For the black babies,

Forget they grow into ugly black adults

Images courtesy of The Sun

The Lost City

We came upon it in the desert quite by chance
There were deep ridges in the earth
The pattern of a giant vegetable plot
Something lay, bared by the force of dry winds
It sparkled intermittently
As the sun's rays bounced off its surface
We wrapped our cotton scarves around our faces
To trap the dust which screamed its passage
Down our throats towards our lungs

Curiosity drove us to walk the red earth
Then dig our fingers deep into unseen crevices
Searching for meaning in the undulations
We struck gold; the old adage
It was useless now, the gold, the adage
Our senses were attuned to the curves and contours

DIMENSIONS

Of earth and rust, of water and air
We heard the scratchy burrowing of small animals

The shimmering was glass reflecting the light
Digging deeper we fell into a chasm
Our bodies slithering down the sides of a ravine
Until our feet touched another layer of red dust
We had landed in a wasteland beneath the wasteland
The earth had lain cracked and bleeding beneath us
Out of sight in pitch coloured darkness
Our torches sliced a pathway through the streets
The stench long gone cleansed by earth upon earth

With that singular light we came upon a signpost

Hanging, still proud above the town
Welcome to Detroit
We had come upon it, in wonderment
That mythological place
Remembered for its fate
Trampled by giants that drank its blood
Crushed its bones, ate its money then left
For better pickings in far away cities

DIMENSIONS

ABOUT THE AUTHOR

Born in Karachi, Pakistan, Shahidah spent her early years in her home village of Malot, in the Jhelum district, before moving to Lahore and then the UK and Ireland. She is the daughter of MK Janjua, the first Commander in Chief of the Pakistani Air Force.

Shahidah is a graduate of the University of Ulster with First Class Honours in Humanities (Majoring in Literature). She has been an activist and writer for 40 years. She was a founding member of the Asian Women's Refuge in Sheffield; a member of the Management Committee of Downtown Women's Centre in Belfast; a founding member of 'Women Into Politics'; co-presented a weekly programme on Belfast Community Radio on issues of violence against women; was an active member of Justice for Women; a member of the Board of Trustees of the UK Rape Crisis Federation, becoming Chairperson in 2003.

In 2003 Shahidah was awarded the Emma Humphreys Memorial Prize. The annual prize of is awarded to an individual woman who has, through writing or campaigning, raised awareness of violence against women and children.

In 2005 Shahidah returned to Ireland to live in Co Kerry, where she continues to live today. She works full time as a writer these days, is a member of the Kerry Women's Interactive Network, and also finds time to volunteer at a couple of local support services.

www.sjanjua.net

Book Cover Review

Philippa Willitts is a freelance writer who writes about feminism, disability rights and injustice with a particular interest in covering and analysing sexual violence, victim blaming and the ways that multiple oppressions intersect. She has been published on the Guardian, Independent, Channel 4 News and New Statesman websites and is a regular contributor to ***the f word*** blog. She lives in Sheffield in the north of England.

www.philippawrites.co.uk

www.ingramcontent.com/pod-product-compliance
Lightning Source LLC
Chambersburg PA
CBHW031500040426
42444CB00007B/1161